VANESSA PLACE

2: Statement of the Case

Statement ~~of Facts~~ is a book about limits and boundaries: physical, psychological, legal, literary, and conceptual. ~~It is~~ about ~~speech and its~~ transcription, and ~~the strange distortions of language that have evolved to serve~~ the legal system. It is about actions that leave a mark ~~on the body and the soul.~~ Most readers will find themselves disoriented and longing to escape ~~from the scarred flesh of~~ this text, but ~~it is a journey worth taking because~~ it reveals just ~~how frail~~ the fabric of justice is.

—Ken Gonzales-Day

By repurposing legal ~~prosecution and defense~~ documents of violent sexual crimes ~~verbatim,~~ *Statement of Facts* takes on issues ~~too messy to benefit from further elucidation which only grow more disturbing~~ presented in their ~~purest~~ case material form. For some, what *Statement of Facts* ~~brings into the public square is salacious, but~~ Place is ~~in effect~~ saying: '~~I move the ball out of this arena and take it into this arena~~' ~~in order to pump up the socio-political volume on this legal/moral battlefield. Her definition of injustice~~ is sweeping. *Statement of Facts* does not care ~~what the reader thinks~~ about content ~~and in essence, Place's relationship to content is like Oprah Winfrey's to money. It is straightforward, and you are free to project onto it whatever you need to. However you respond to this fierce book,~~ it is indisputable that *Statement of Facts* has ~~carved out~~ a place for itself as a touchstone of poetic ~~push-back. As Pasadena Superior Court Judge Gilbert Alston famously quipped in his~~ dismissal of ~~a 1986 rape case because the victim was a prostitute:~~ 'A whore is a whore is a whore'—*Statement of Facts* counters by unflinchingly reminding us 'a rape is a rape is a rape.'

—Kim Rosenfield

~~*Statement of Facts* is poet/lawyer Vanessa Place's masterful demonstration of day-for-night writing. Alternately nauseating, cold, gripping, philosophical, and relentless,~~ this volume is an analytical portrait of a writer writing in double-time, simultaneously producing legal language caught in the trap of trying (and failing) to secure the self-evident meanings of ~~the factual, and poetic~~ language procedurally ~~measuring the way facts are fundamentally also instruments of violence,~~ building toward the legitimation of a legal edifice ~~from which no one can escape.~~ These descriptions ~~of heinous sex crimes,~~ detached from their original function ~~as depositions,~~ are a treatise on contingency; a discourse on the moral lenses ~~of narrative; and an institutional critique~~ of the aesthetics and ethics of juridical administration.

—Simon Leung

Vanessa Place is ~~a lawyer and,~~ like Bartelby, ~~much of~~ her work involves ~~scribing appellate briefs, that task of~~ copying and editing, rendering ~~complex lives and dirty deeds into "neutral"~~ language ~~to be~~ presented before a court. That is her ~~day job. Her~~ poetry ~~is an appropriation of the documents she writes during her day job, flipping her briefs after hours into literature. And~~ like most literature, they're chock full of ~~high drama, pathos, horror and humanity. But unlike most literature, she hasn't written a word of it. Or has she? Here's where it gets interesting. She both has written them and, at the same time, she's wholly appropriated them—rescuing them from~~ the dreary world ~~of court filings and bureaucracy—and, by mere reframing, turns them into what is~~ arguably the most challenging, complex and controversial literature ~~being~~ written today.

—Kenneth Goldsmith

VANESSA PLACE

Tragodía
2: Statement of the Case

Blanc Press
Los Angeles, California

TRAGODÍA 2: STATEMENT OF THE CASE
Blanc Press June, 2011
Los Angeles, California
© 2011 Vanessa Place
ISBN: 978-1-934254-26-4

A portion of *Statement of the Case* appeared in ArcheTime: Cross-Disciplinary Conference and Exhibition, June 4-14, 2009 at the Tank Space, New York City.

Vanessa Place would like to thank Kenneth Goldsmith, Marjorie Perloff, Robert Fitterman, Kim Rosenfield, Teresa Carmody and Mathew Timmons.

All quotations and accounts in this book were taken directly from the trial transcripts of cases that Vanessa Place handled on appeal. All these transcripts, and the appellate briefs filed in each case, are matters of public record. However, the names of the people herein, as well as other direct modes of identification, have been changed to protect their privacy.

Blanc Press Los Angeles
Freedom of the press is limited to those who own one.
When the rim is bent it will press against the works and
impede the proper action of the currents.
blancpress.com

TABLE OF CONTENTS

1. STATEMENT OF THE CASE 9
2. STATEMENT OF THE CASE 11
3. STATEMENT OF THE CASE 13
4. STATEMENT OF THE CASE 15
5. STATEMENT OF THE CASE 17
6. STATEMENT OF THE CASE 19
7. STATEMENT OF THE CASE 21
8. STATEMENT OF THE CASE 23
9. STATEMENT OF THE CASE 25
10. STATEMENT OF THE CASE 27
11. STATEMENT OF THE CASE 29
12. STATEMENT OF THE CASE 31
13. STATEMENT OF THE CASE 33
14. STATEMENT OF THE CASE 35
15. STATEMENT OF THE CASE 37
16. STATEMENT OF THE CASE 39
17. STATEMENT OF THE CASE 41
18. STATEMENT OF THE CASE 43
19. STATEMENT OF THE CASE 49
20. STATEMENT OF THE CASE 51
21. STATEMENT OF THE CASE 53

22. STATEMENT OF THE CASE 55

23. STATEMENT OF THE CASE 57

24. STATEMENT OF THE CASE 59

25. STATEMENT OF THE CASE 61

26. STATEMENT OF THE CASE 63

27. STATEMENT OF THE CASE 65

28. STATEMENT OF THE CASE 67

29. STATEMENT OF THE CASE 69

30. STATEMENT OF THE CASE 71

31. STATEMENT OF THE CASE 73

32. STATEMENT OF THE CASE 75

33. STATEMENT OF THE CASE 79

Tragodia 2: Statement of the Case

STATEMENT OF THE CASE

An amended information charged appellant with aggravated sexual assault of a child (count 1, Pen. Code § 269(a)(1)), forcible child molestation (counts 2-11, Pen. Code § 288(b)(1)), failure to register (count 12, Pen. Code § 290(g)(2)), and aggravated sexual assault of a child - oral copulation (count 13, Pen. Code § 269(a)(4)); Penal Code section 667.61, subdivisions (a) and (d) prior conviction and subdivision (b) multiple victim allegations were alleged as to all counts, as was a Penal Code section 667, subdivision (a)(1) prior conviction enhancement. Appellant pled not guilty. (CT 70-83)

Over objection, the court granted the State's motion to admit prior uncharged offense and disposition evidence pursuant to Evidence Code sections 1101, subdivision (b) and 1108. (CT 94-105, 109-120; RT 2-5)

During deliberations, the jury sent a note indicating they were divided eight guilty and four not guilty on count 1, had found appellant unanimously guilty on counts 2 through 12, and not guilty on count 13. (CT 137; RT 1501-1506, 1801) The verdicts were in accordance; the jury furthermore found the prior conviction allegations true, and the multiple victim allegation not true. A mistrial was declared as to count 1. (CT 189-215, 217-219; RT 1507-1517)

Appellant was sentenced to a total of 221 years to life: count 2 - the upper term of 8 years, doubled as a second strike, in addition to 25 years to life, also doubled as a second strike, plus 5 years pursuant to section 667, subdivision (a); count 3 - the upper term of 8 years, doubled as a second strike; count 4 - the upper term of 8 years, doubled; count 5 - the upper term of 8 years, doubled; count 6 - the upper term of 8 years, doubled; count 7 - the upper term of 8 years, doubled; count 8 - the upper term of 8 years, doubled; count 9 - the upper term of 8 years, doubled; count 10 - the upper term of 8 years, doubled; count 11 - the upper term of 8 years, doubled; count 12 - the upper term of 3 years, doubled; all counts were run consecutively. Appellant was credited with 626 days precommittment confinement, including 208 days conduct credit. (CT 229-236; RT 1829-1830)

This appeal from a final judgment of conviction is timely. (CT 237-238)

VANESSA PLACE

Tragodia 2: Statement of the Case

STATEMENT OF THE CASE

An information was filed charging appellant with rape in concert (count 1, Pen. Code § 264.1), rape by foreign object in concert (count 2, Pen. Code § 264.1), street terrorism (count 3, Pen. Code § 186.22), and unlawful sexual intercourse (count 4, Pen. Code § 261.5(c)). A Penal Code section 186.22, subdivision (b)(1) gang enhancement was alleged as to counts 1 and 2.[1] Appellant pled not guilty. (CT 1:30-34, 1:37)

A defense pretrial motion to bifurcate the gang allegations was denied; an Evidence Code section 352 motion to exclude gang evidence was also denied during trial. (CT 1:92, 1:130) During voir dire, appellant's counsel moved to dismiss the venire pursuant to *People v. Wheeler* (1978) 22 Cal.3d 258; after finding *Wheeler* error, the court kept the improperly-challenged juror on the panel. (CT 1:112; Aug. RT 3:498) Pretrial, defense counsel for co-defendant moved to exclude references to co-defendant and defense witnesses' criminal histories, including charges and accusations, to sever the gang allegations from the other charges, and to admit evidence of a prior false accusation by one of the victims. The prosecutor's trial brief argued for admission of expert gang testimony and exclusion of evidence of the victims' sexual histories. (2nd Aug. CT 1:1-3, 19-43, 44-56, 57-60; RT 1:20-26) During trial, co-counsel moved to preclude admission of gang evidence pursuant to Evidence Code section 352 after the victim testified the assault was not gang-related. The court denied the motion. (RT 3:469-470) Throughout the trial, particularly during the gang expert's testimony, there were numerous objections to gang evidence on relevance, prejudice, hearsay and foundational grounds. (RT 3:637, 4:710, 4:712, 4:769)

During deliberations, the jury sent a note pointing out that the instructions indicated the People had to prove the crime was committed "for the benefit of, at the direction of [or] in association w/gang" while the verdict forms said the crime had to be "committed for the benefit of, at the direction of [and] in association with a criminal street gang," asking which was the proper conjunctive. The court responded in writing that "The answer is 'or'." (CT 2:221-224; RT 5:1032-1033)

Appellant was found guilty as charged; the gang enhancement was found true. (CT 2:198-205, 2:225; RT 5:1034-1039) The court denied a motion for new trial, and appellant was sentenced to a total of 20 years: count 1 - the midterm of 7 years, plus 10 years pursuant to section 186.22, served consecutively; count 2 - one-third the midterm of 28 months, served

---

[1] Appellant's co-defendants were also charged in counts 1, 2, and 3. (CT 1:32-34)

consecutively; count 3 - the midterm of 2 years, served concurrently; and count 4 - one-third the midterm of 8 months, served consecutively. The count 2 section 186.22 allegation was stricken under section 1385. Appellant was credited with 432 days precommitment confinement, including 56 days conduct credit. (CT 2:261-267; CT1:1-12; RT 5:1050, 5:1058-1059, 5:1082-1085)

This appeal from a final judgment of conviction is timely. (CT 2:268)

Tragodia 2: Statement of the Case

STATEMENT OF THE CASE

An information charged appellant with child molestation (Pen. Code § 288(c)(1)); prior robbery, rape, and assault with a deadly weapon convictions were alleged pursuant to Penal Code sections 1170.12, subdivision (a) through (d), and 667, subdivision (a)(1); a prior petty theft conviction was alleged under section 667.5, subdivision (b). After the State's motion to strike the section 667, subdivision (a)(1) allegations was granted, appellant pled not guilty and denied the remaining allegations. (CT 140-143)

Pretrial, counsel moved to exclude evidence of other conduct proffered under Evidence Code sections 1101 and 1108; the court reserved ruling on the motion. Counsel later renewed the motion, and the court again reserved ruling, but indicated it felt the evidence was probative as to intent, plan and lack of mistake/accident. Before instruction and argument, counsel objected to CALJIC No. 2.50.1; the court then excluded the evidence under section 1108, but found the testimony admissible under section 1101, subdivision (b) on the points specified. (CT 367-397, 419-445, 454; RT E-4-E-5, 10-18, 913-918, 1881-1889)

During deliberations, the jury requested the closing argument diagram and readback of the victim's testimony, refining that request to that part of the testimony "from the 1st touching to the 4th touch." In a subsequent note, the jury asked for readback of the victim's testimony regarding "alleged 'contact' at the park." (CT 459-460, 462-463) The panel then asked for readback of the detective's testimony regarding the preparation and presentation of the photographic lineup. (CT 461) The jury also wanted the large display of the park, but the court denied this request as the display was not in evidence. (CT 464)

Appellant was found guilty as charged. (CT 516-518; RT 2702-2703) Appellant waived jury trial on his prior convictions; following a court trial, the enhancement allegations were found true as alleged. (CT 518, 533-538, 652; RT-2703-2704, 3309-3310) The court struck the robbery and assault priors pursuant to *People v. Superior Court (Romero)* (1996) 13 Cal.4th 497, sentencing appellant to a total of 7 years in state prison: the upper term of 3 years, doubled as a second strike, plus one year for the section 667.5, subdivision (b) allegation. Appellant was credited with 771 days precommitment confinement, including 257 days conduct credit. (CT 654-655; RT 3319-3322)

This appeal from a final judgment of conviction is timely. (CT 656-658)

Tragodia 2: Statement of the Case

STATEMENT OF THE CASE

An amended information charged appellant with forcible oral copulation (count 1, Pen. Code § 288a(c)(2)), false imprisonment by violence (count 2, Pen. Code § 236), and criminal threats (count 3, Pen. Code § 422). A prior Penal Code section 288, subdivision (b) conviction was alleged as to count 1 pursuant to sections 667.61, subdivisions (a) and (d) and 667.71, as well as a section 667.61, subdivision (b) knife use allegation. Two prior convictions were alleged to all counts under sections 1170.12, subdivisions (a) through (d), 667, subdivisions (b) through (l), 667, subdivision (a)(1), and 667.5, subdivision (b). Following the appropriate advisements and waivers, appellant's motion to proceed in propria persona was granted; appellant then pled not guilty. (CT 154-159, 93-94; RT A-1-A-9, A-15, 14-16)

Over repeated defense objection, the court admitted evidence of prior sex offenses pursuant to section 1108. (CT 130-133, 159, Supp. CT 15-18; RT 18, 21-28, 312, 626, 931-934, 1250, 2103-2105) Appellant ultimately refused to participate in the prior offense portion of the trial, citing in part, the fact the prior offense was currently being litigated before the Ninth Circuit Court of Appeal; the court instructed the jury to disregard this information, as well as appellant's statement that he had never been convicted of any offense relative to one of the section 1108 witnesses. (RT 1241, 1247-1250, 1252)

During deliberations, the jury requested readback of various testimony regarding the use of a knife. (CT 185; RT 2771-2772, 3017) The jury was unable to reach a verdict on the weapon allegation, and the court declared a mistrial as to that allegation. Appellant was otherwise found guilty as charged. (CT 188-190; RT 3019-3025)

The priors allegations were found true as alleged.[1] (CT 287-293; RT 3605-3610) Citing California Rules of Court, rule 4.421(a),(b) the sentencing court found as factors in aggravation that the crime involved great violence, great bodily harm, threat of great bodily harm, or other acts disclosing a high degree of cruelty, viciousness, or callousness, that appellant had engaged in a pattern of violent conduct demonstrating a serious danger to society, his prior convictions were numerous or of increasing seriousness, he had served prior prison terms, was on parole at the time of the current offense, and his prior performance on probation/parole was unsatisfactory. Appellant was sentenced

---

[1] During jury instruction in the priors trial, appellant interrupted the court to demand his sentencing transcripts. Outside the presence of the jury, the court found appellant's disruption warranted restraints under section 1043; the court subsequently admonished the jury to disregard appellant.s behavior. (CT 191-193; RT 3112, 3301-3312)

to a total of 85 years to life: count 1 - the upper term of 25 years to life, pursuant to section 667.61, subdivision (h)[2], tripled as a third strike, plus five years for each section 667, subdivision (a)(1) allegation; count 2 - the upper term of 3 years, tripled to 9 years, stayed pursuant to section 654; count 3 - the upper term of 3 years, tripled to 9 years, stayed under section 654; the section 667.5, subdivision (b) terms were stayed. Appellant was credited with 201 days precommitment confinement, including 26 days conduct credit. (CT 333-338; RT 3316-3318, 3635, 3655-3663)

Permission to file a belated notice of appeal was granted by this Court on May 18, 2004; a notice of appeal was subsequently timely filed. (CT 339-341)

---

2   In choosing to exercise its option to sentence alternatively under section 667.61, subdivision (h), the court struck the section 667.71 allegation/verdict. The court found the offenses in counts 2 and 3 incidental to the offense charged as count 1. (CT 334; RT 3656-3657)

STATEMENT OF THE CASE

An amended information charged appellant and codefendant with kidnaping to commit robbery (count 1, Pen. Code § 209(b)(1)), assault with a firearm (counts 2 and 6, Pen. Code § 245(a)(2)); appellant was additionally charged with forcible oral copulation (counts 3, 4, and 5, Pen. Code § 288a(c)(2)), possession of a firearm by an ex-felon (count 7, Pen. Code § 12021(a)(1)), and failure to file a change of address (count 9, Pen. Code § 290(f)(1)). As to appellant, Penal Code sections 12022.5, subdivision (a)(1) and 12022.53, subdivision (b) weapon use allegations were alleged on count 1; a section 12022.5 weapon use allegation made as to counts 2 and 6, section 12022.3, subdivision (a) weapon use allegations and section 667.61, subdivisions (a) and (d) kidnaping allegations as to counts 3, 4, and 5. A Penal Code section 667, subdivisions (b) through (l) allegation was made as to all counts, based on appellant's five counts of conviction in Case No. A593983; a section 667, subdivision (a)(1) allegation stemming from the same case was made on counts 1 through 6.[1] Appellant pled not guilty. (CT 153-163, 307)

Pretrial, the State moved for admission of evidence of prior sexual offenses pursuant to Evidence Code sections 1101, subdivision (b) and 1108, over defense objection. The court found the previous crimes admissible under both sections. (CT 230-251; RT 12-19, 21-30) The court granted appellant's motion to bifurcate the priors and count 9, and, following the appropriate advisements and waivers, appellant admitted his prior conviction relative to the ex-felon in possession charge. Appellant later waived his right to jury trial on count 9 after the verdicts on the other counts were heard. (CT 262-263, 394; RT 2, 8-11, 32-36, 39-40, 3916-3917, 3919-3921) During trial, the court excluded evidence the victim had an outstanding prostitution warrant at the time she made her accusations against appellant. (RT 1288-1290)

Appellant was found guilty of kidnaping as a lesser offense to count 1, the weapon use allegation was found true. Appellant was otherwise found guilty as charged, the weapon use allegations charged in counts 2, 3, 4, 5, 6, were found true, as was the kidnaping allegation in counts 3, 4, and 5. (CT 382, 389, 393-397; RT 3904-3911) Following the appropriate advisements and waivers,

---

[1] Codefendant was additionally charged with cocaine possession (count 8, Health & Saf. Code § 11350(a)); weapons use allegations were made as to her on count 2.(CT 153) Codefendant was convicted of kidnaping and possession and sentenced to a total of 3 years: 3 years on count 1, 2 years on count 8, run concurrent. Codefendant filed an appeal in *People v. Hagens*, 2d District Court of Appeal Case No. B14287; a Motion to Abate Appeal Upon Death of Appellant was filed on July 8, 2002. This Court filed an order of dismissal on August 16, 2002.

appellant admitted his prior convictions pursuant to section 667, subdivision (a) (1). (CT 485-486; RT 4217-4219)

Defense counsel filed a motion for new trial based on newly discovered evidence: a declaration by one of the percipient witnesses stating appellant did not break into the motel room and that the victim voluntarily left the room with appellant. The court denied the motion. A supplemental motion for new trial was filed based on the victim's repudiation of her trial testimony and her explanation that her testimony had been dictated by police reports; after hearing and argument, the court denied the motion. (CT 434-449, 485, 494-496, 505, 507-508, 525; RT 4201-4215, 4810)

Appellant was sentenced to a total of 230 years to life: count 1 - 25 years to life plus the upper term of 10 years for the section 12022.53, subdivision (b) allegation and 5 years for the section 667, subdivision (a) enhancement, stayed pursuant to section 654; count 2 - 40 years to life: 15 years to life plus the upper term of 10 years for the weapon enhancement and 5 years for the prior conviction allegation; count 3 - 85 years to life: 25 years to life tripled pursuant to section 667, subdivision (e)(2), plus the upper term of 10 years for the weapons use allegation and 5 years for the prior conviction allegation, the 5 year prior stayed pursuant to section 654; count 4 - 35 years to life: 25 years to life plus 10 years for the weapons use, the 5 year prior stayed; count 5 - 35 years to life: 25 years to life plus 10 years for the weapons use, the 5 year prior stayed; count 6 - 35 years to life: 25 to life plus 10 for the weapons use allegation, the 5 year prior stayed; count 7 - 25 years to life stayed under section 654.[2] Appellant was credited with 2,436 days precommittment confinement, including 812 days conduct credit. (CT 553-555; Supp. CT 1-4; RT 5102-5107)

This appeal from a judgment of conviction is timely. (CT 552)

---

2   The State dismissed all other allegations. (Supp. CT 4)

Tragodia 2: Statement of the Case

STATEMENT OF THE CASE

An information charged appellant with child molestation (counts 1 and 2, Pen. Code § 288, subdivision (a)). Appellant pleaded not guilty. (CT 4-5, 10)

Counsel made a motion in limine to exclude prior offense evidence; the State made a "motion in limine to impeach" appellant with "moral turpitude conduct." The court granted the State's motion. (CT 65-78, 95-99-1, 101; RT 35-44)

During deliberations, the jury requested readback of the victim's testimony, the first day's testimony of Sylvia, and a "breakdown of count 1 and 2." Readback was permitted, and the court's written response to the "breakdown" request was that count 1 was based on the allegation appellant touched the victim's breasts while tracing letters on her shirt, and count 2 on the allegation he touched her chest while reaching into the candy box. (CT 178)

Appellant was found guilty as charged. (CT 180-184, 186-187; RT 343-345) Appellant was placed on forty-eight months formal probation, the conditions of which included serving 365 days in county jail, payment of $400.00 in restitution, and a fine of $200.00 pursuant to Penal Code section 290.3, and registration under section 290. (CT 216-219; RT 358-361)

This appeal from a final judgment of conviction is timely. (CT 220)

Tragodia 2: Statement of the Case

STATEMENT OF THE CASE

An information was filed charging appellant with aggravated sexual assault of a child (rape) (counts 1 and 2, Pen. Code § 269(a)(1)); forcible rape (counts 3 and 4, Pen. Code § 261(a)(2)); forcible oral copulation (counts 5 and 6, Pen. Code § 288a(c)(2)), forcible sodomy (count 7, Pen. Code § 286(c)(2)); and continuous sexual abuse (count 8, Pen. Code § 288.5(a)).[1] (CT 7-16) Appellant pled not guilty. (CT 17)

During trial, the victim/witness was admonished about the consequences of perjury, and an attorney appointed to represent her during her testimony. The witness was subsequently impeached with her preliminary hearing testimony under *People v. Green* (1971) 3 Cal.3d 981. (RT 1:156-160, 1:163-175, 188-201) The prosecutor also apparently "choked up" during his opening statement. (RT 1:130-132)

Appellant was found guilty as charged. (CT 125-135; RT 4:809-812) A motion for new trial was made based on juror misconduct, prosecutorial misconduct, erroneous admission of the DNA evidence, and insufficient evidence; the court denied the motion. (CT 154-168; RT 4: 820-826) Appellant was sentenced to a total of 72 years to life: count 1 - 15 years to life; count 2 - 15 years to life, run consecutively; count 3 - the midterm of 6 years, run consecutively; count 3 - the midterm of 6 years, run consecutively; count 4 - the midterm of 6 years, run consecutively; count 5 - the midterm of 6 years, run consecutively; count 6 - the midterm of 6 years, run consecutively; count 7 - the midterm of 6 years, run consecutively; and count 8 - the midterm of 12 years, run consecutively. Appellant was credited with 638 days precommitment confinement, with no conduct credit. (CT 182-188; RT 4:853-856)

This appeal from a final judgment of conviction is timely.

---

[1] The time frames alleged were: counts 1 and 2 - August 30, 2001 to August 29, 2003; counts 3 through 6 - August 30, 2003 to August 29, 2005; count 7 - August 30, 2002 to August 29, 2005; and count 8 - August 30, 1997 to August 29, 2001. (CT 8-15)

Tragodia 2: Statement of the Case

STATEMENT OF THE CASE

An amended information charged appellant with eight counts of child molestation (counts 1-8, Pen. Code § 288(a)); it was further alleged pursuant to *Blakely v. Washington* (2004) 542 U.S. 296 that the victim was particularly vulnerable because she was five or six years old, and the defendant took advantage of a position of trust to commit the offense as he lived with the victim, the offense was committed in the residence, and the defendant occupied the role of the victim's father. Appellant pled not guilty. (CT 39-40, 54-61; RT 616)

At the request of both parties, the court admitted evidence appellant had taken, and failed, a polygraph examination. (RT 602-603) During argument, the prosecutor contended the results of the polygraph proved appellant was lying about not molesting the victim; there was no objection, and the jury was not given a limiting instruction not to consider the polygraph results in assessing appellant's credibility. (RT 1882-1884)

Appellant was found guilty as charged. (CT 148-158; RT 2103-2106) Appellant was sentenced to a total of 20 years: count 1 - the midterm of 6 years; count 2 - one-third the midterm of 2 years, run consecutive; count 3 - one-third the midterm of 2 years, run consecutive; count 4 - one-third the midterm of 2 years, run consecutive; count 5 - one-third the midterm of 2 years, run consecutive; count 6 - one-third the midterm of 2 years, run consecutive; count 7 - one-third the midterm of 2 years, run consecutive; and count 8 - one-third the midterm of 2 years, run consecutive. The terms were run consecutively pursuant to Penal Code section 667.5, subdivision (c)(6) as involving separate incidents with the same victim. Appellant was credited with 266 days precommitment confinement, including 35 days conduct credit. (CT 165-169; RT 2402-2403, 2407-2408)

This appeal from a final judgment of conviction is timely. (CT 170)

VANESSA PLACE

Tragodia 2: Statement of the Case

STATEMENT OF THE CASE

An amended information was filed charging appellant with rape of an unconscious person (count 1, Pen. Code § 261 (a)(4)), forcible oral copulation (count 2, Pen. Code § 288a(c)(2)), forcible rape (counts 3 and 6, Pen. Code § 261(a)(2)), sexual penetration by foreign object (counts 4 and 7, Pen. Code § 289(a)), and false imprisonment by violence (count 5, Pen. Code § 236).[1] A prior rape conviction was alleged pursuant to Penal Code section 667.61, subdivisions (a)(b) and (d)(1) as to counts 2, 3, 4, 6 and 7. Prior attempted oral copulation, rape and kidnapping convictions were alleged pursuant to Penal Code section 667.71 as to counts 3 and 6. A Penal Code section 667.61, subdivisions (a),(b) and (e)(5) multiple victim allegations and subdivisions (a), (b) and (e)(6) tying and binding allegations were made as to counts 2, 3, 4, 6 and 7. Prior assault with a deadly weapon/by means of force likely to cause great bodily injury, kidnapping, attempted oral copulation convictions were alleged on all counts pursuant to Penal Code section 1170, subdivisions (a) through (d), and on counts 1, 2, 3, 4, 5 and 6 pursuant to section 667, subdivision (a)(1). A Penal Code section 667.5, subdivision (b) prior prison sentence allegation was also made as to all counts. Appellant pleaded not guilty. (CT 1:169-177; RT 1:5)

Pretrial, appellant objected to admission of testimony about a sexual assault examination by someone other than the person who performed the exam. The court overruled the objection. (RT 1:12-15)

Following the appropriate advisements, appellant waived his right to a jury trial on the prior allegations, which were bifurcated from the trial. (CT 2:193, 2:206; RT 2:62-64; RT 6:1158-1161) During deliberations, the jury asked for the definition of "binding." (CT 2:291) The panel subsequently sent a note stating the jury instructions on counts 3 and 6 did not mention tying and binding, though the verdict forms did. They again requested the "legal definition" of tying/binding. The court wrote that there was no legal definition, and to use the common ordinary meaning of the words. (CT 2:292) The jury requested a readback of Renee's testimony. (CT 2:293, 2:301) They also asked for the police reports and readback of Lisa's testimony regarding the bag over her head. The court indicated the police reports were not exhibits. (CT 2:294, 2:301)

Appellant was found guilty of counts 1 through 6[2]; the multiple victim allegation and tying/binding allegations were found not true on counts 2 and 4,

---

1   Counts 1 through 5 alleged violations occurring on May 8, 2005 against Renee; counts 6 and 7 alleged violations occurring on December 12, 2004 against Lisa. (CT 1: 170-173)

2   Count 7 was previously dismissed. (RT 7:1292)

true on count 3; the multiple victim allegation was found true on count 6, the tying/binding allegation true on count 6. (CT 2:295-304; RT 7:1248-1253) Following a court trial on the priors, the court found the strike allegations true as to the prior sex offenses and not true as to the prior assault conviction. Appellant's motion for self-representation was granted for sentencing/post-sentencing, and subsequently withdrawn. New counsel appointed for sentencing/post-sentencing. (CT 2:324, 2:327-330; RT 7:1248, 7:1277, 7:1292-1293) Appellant's subsequent motion for new trial was denied. (CT 2:329, 2:354; RT 7:1278, 7:1282, 7:1299-1300)

Appellant was sentenced to a total of 230 years to life: count 1 – 25 years to life; count 2 – 25 years to life; count 3 – 80 years to life based on the multiple victim and tying/binding allegations, plus 5 years for the prior serious felony allegation; count 4 – 25 years to lie; count 5 – 25 years to life; and count 6 – 50 years to life based on the section 667.61 subdivisions (a) and (e) allegations, run consecutively pursuant to section 667.6, subdivision (d). Counts 1, 2, 4 and 5 were run consecutively as based on separate acts of violence committed on separate occasions. Appellant was credited with 1,409 days precommitment confinement, including 184 days conduct credit. (CT 2:354-360; RT 7:1300-1303)

This appeal from a final judgment of conviction is timely. (CT 2:361-362)

Tragodia 2: Statement of the Case

STATEMENT OF THE CASE

An amended information was filed charging appellant with assault to commit sex offenses (counts 1, 4, 11 and 16, Pen. Code § 220), burglary (counts 2, 3, 12, and 13, Pen. Code § 459), child annoyance (counts 5, 6, 7 and 8, Pen. Code § 647.6), attempted aggravated kidnapping (count 9, Pen. Code §§ 664/209 (b)), sexual battery (count 10, Pen. Code § 243.4 (e)(1)) forcible sexual penetration by a foreign object (count 14, Pen. Code § 289 (a)(1)); and attempted rape (count 15, Pen. Code §§ 664/261 (a)(2)).[1] A Penal Code sections 1170.12, subdivisions (a) through (d) and 667, subdivision (a)(1) prior assault with a firearm conviction was alleged as to all counts. A section 667.61, subdivisions (a)(d) burglary allegation was made as to count 14. Appellant pled not guilty. (CT 1:287-288, 2:480-492, 2:506-507; RT 2:E-8, 6:3302)

On March 9, 2007, appellant was involuntarily committed pursuant to Penal Code section 1368. (CT 2:315-316; RT 2:D-5) On January 11, 2008, appellant was found competent to stand trial. (CT 2:325-326; RT 2:E-2, E-7)

During deliberations, the jury sent a note requesting clarification, or "legal definitions" of "assault with intent to commit a rape & attempted forcible rape." The court wrote in response that assault with intent to commit rape is a greater offense to the lesser crime of attempted forcible rape, referring the panel to the instructions. (CT 2:396-398) A second note indicated that the jury agreed appellant was guilty of simple assault, but could not agree if appellant was guilty of the greater offenses. The court cited CALCRIM 3517 to the effect that it was up to the jury to decide the order in which it reached its decisions, but that the court could accept a verdict of guilty on a lesser offense only if the jury has found the defendant not guilty of the greater. (CT 2:399; RT 6:2404-2407; RT 6:2701-2705) A third note requested readback of the testimony of Pergroghi, Darlita, and Vanoush. (CT 2:400-402; 6:2706, 6:2709)

Appellant was found guilty as charged on counts 1, 2, 3, 5, 6, 7, 8, 9, 10, 11, 12, 13, 14, 15 and 16. A mistrial was declared as to count 4. (CT 2:436-457; RT 6:3002, 6:3007-3011, 6:3015) In a bifurcated proceeding, the court found appellant's prior convictions true as alleged. (CT 2:507; RT 6:3304, 6:3334-3335) Appellant's motion to strike his prior conviction was denied. (CT

---

1   Counts 1 and 2 alleged violations occurring on March 11, 2005 against Tonia; count 3 was against Jason on March 11, 2005; count 4 against Pergrouhi on March 7, 2005; count 5 against Kathryn on March 11, 2005; count 6 against Ysabel on March 11, 2005; count 7 against Keran on March 11, 2005; count 8 against Sara on March 11, 2005; counts 9 and 11 against Maragret on March 20, 2004; count 10 against Marem on March 11, 2005; count 12 against L. S. [sic] on March 11, 2005; and counts 12 through 16 against Natay (sic) on February 20, 2005.

2:561; RT 6:3617-3621) Appellant was sentenced to a total of 170 years to life: count 1 – 25 years to life, plus 5 years for the prior conviction allegation, run consecutive; count 2 - 25 years to life, plus 5 years, run concurrent; count 3 – 25 years to life, plus 5 years, run consecutive; count 5 – 1 year, run consecutive; count 6 – 1 year, run concurrent; count 7 – 1 year, run concurrent; count 8 – 1 year, run consecutive; count 9 – 25 years to life, run consecutive; count 10 – 6 months, run consecutive; count 11 – 25 years to life, stayed pursuant to section 654; count 12 – 25 years to life, plus 5 years, run concurrent; count 13 – 25 years to life, plus 5 years, run concurrent; count 14 – 75 years to life, plus 5 years, run consecutive; count 15 – 25 years to life, plus 5 years, run concurrent; and count 16 – 25 years to life, plus 5 years, run concurrent. Appellant was credited with 1,468 days precomittment confinement, including 162 days conduct credit. (CT 2:563-575; RT 6:3621, 6:3624-3635)

This appeal from a final judgment of conviction is timely. (CT 2:576)

STATEMENT OF THE CASE

On June 16, 2003, the District Attorney of Ventura County filed an amended petition alleging appellant was a Sexually Violent Predator (SVP) pursuant to Welfare & Institutions Code section 6600. The petition alleged appellant had been convicted of two sexually violent offenses within the meaning of sections 6600, subdivision (b), and 6600.1, subdivision (a): five counts of oral copulation of an unconscious person, in violation of Penal Code section 288a(f), involving two separate victims.[1] (CT 72-77) The petition further alleged that, based on evaluations by the Department of Mental Health (DMH) incorporated in the original petition,[2] appellant had a diagnosed mental disorder such that he was likely to engage in acts of sexual violence without appropriate treatment and custody. (CT 1-61, 73)

A probable cause hearing was set for June 16, 2003; the court denied appellant's request to be returned to Atascadero State Hospital to retain private counsel, found probable cause, and held appellant over for trial. (CT 63, 82; RT 127-128)

Jury trial began on December 4, 2003; on December 12, 2003, the jury found appellant met the SVP criteria as defined in sections 6600 through 6604. (CT 233, 286, 288; RT 192-I-192-L, 839-841) Appellant was committed to the California Department of Mental Health. (CT 286; RT 842-843)

This appeal from an order of commitment is timely. (CT 289)

---

[1] (Case No. CR-29232.)

[2] Filed April 9, 2003. (CT 1)

Tragodia 2: Statement of the Case

STATEMENT OF THE CASE

An amended information charged appellant with rape (counts 1, 2 and 3, Pen. Code § 261(a)(2); a Penal Code section 12022.8 great bodily injury allegation was made as to all counts,[1] as was a prior rape conviction allegation under sections 1170.12, subdivision (a) through (d) and 667, subdivision (b) through (l), and a section 667.5, subdivision (b) prior prison term allegation. It was further alleged under California Rules of Court, rule 4.421(a)(3) that the victim was particularly vulnerable, and under rule 4.421(a)(4) that appellant induced others to participate in the crime and occupied a position of leadership/dominance in its commission.[2]

Appellant pled not guilty, and a request to strike the strike allegations subsequently granted. (CT 83, 139-144)

The jury was instructed under CALJIC No. 1.23.1 ["Consent" - Defined in Rape, Sodomy, Unlawful Penetration and Oral Copulation]. (CT 166; RT 1509)

Appellant was found guilty as charged; the rule 4.421(a)(3) allegation was found true. (CT 206-211; RT 1801-1805) Appellant was sentenced to a total of 24 years: count 1 - the upper term of 8 years, count 2 - the upper term of 8 years, run consecutive, and count 3 - the upper term of 8 years, run consecutive. The court found as factors in aggravation that the victim was fifteen years old at the time and was under the influence of alcohol and/or drugs; the court sentenced consecutively under section 667.6, subdivision (d), but noted that if it had discretion, it would impose consecutive terms as there were three separate rapes involving three separate men. Appellant was credited with 380 days precommitment confinement, including 50 days conduct credit. (CT 220-223; RT 2102, 2106-2108)

This appeal from a final judgment of conviction is timely. (CT 224)

---

1 Pretrial, the State dismissed the section 12022.8 and prior conviction allegations. (RT 301, 308)

2 Pursuant to section 995, the court dismissed the rule 4.421(a)(4) allegation; the court refused a defense request to bifurcate the rest of the *Blakely* allegations. (RT 302, 306-307)

STATEMENT OF THE CASE

An information charged appellant with child molestation (counts 1, 2, 3, and 4, Pen. Code § 288(c)(1) [accused at least ten years older than victim]), and oral copulation of a person under the age of sixteen (counts 5, 6, and 7, Pen. Code § 288a(b)(2)). Appellant pleaded not guilty. (CT 55-62)

During deliberations, the jury asked for an explanation of the difference between counts 5 and 6, noting there were no dates on the verdict forms for counts 1 through 4, though they understood the dates were "Count 1 - 1-1-04 through 2-29-04, Count 2 - 3-1-04 through 4-30-04, Count 3 - 5-1-04 through 5-31-04, Count 4 - 6-01-04 through 6-24-04." The court's written response stated that the People had alleged two separate incidents of oral copulation occurred during this period, "Hence 2 counts," and that the jury's dates were correct. A second note asked for readback of Esme's testimony regarding the "butt plug." A third note asked for readback of Waverly's testimony about the sleeping arrangements for the evening before the January 2004 trip to San Diego. A fourth note asked where were Defense Exhibits A, B and C; the court wrote that they were not admitted into evidence. A fifth note asked for all testimony regarding "sodomy anal butt sex by any and all witnesses." A sixth note stated the jury was deadlocked on count 7, and believed further deliberation would not resolve the impasse; the court's written response asked if further instruction would help; the jury said no further instruction was needed. (CT 211-216; RT 3:789-792)

Appellant was found guilty on counts 1 through 6. (CT 217-225; RT 3:793-796) Represented by substitute counsel, appellant filed a motion for new trial based on ineffective assistance of trial counsel; the motion was denied. (CT 236-283, 296-297; RT 3:801-802, 811-812) Appellant was sentenced to a total of 5 years, 4 months: count 1 - the midterm of 2 years; count 2 - one-third the midterm of 8 months; count 3 - one-third the midterm of 8 months; count 4 - one-third the midterm of 8 months; count 5 - one-third the midterm of 8 months; count 6 - one-third the midterm of 8 months.[1] Appellant was credited with 270 days precommitment confinement, including 90 days conduct credit. (CT 297-301; RT 3:816-821)

This appeal from a final judgment of conviction is timely. (CT 302)

---

1 Count 7 was dismissed under section 1385. (CT 299)

STATEMENT OF THE CASE

An amended information charged appellant with continuous sexual abuse (count 1, Pen. Code §288.5(a)); a Penal Code section 803, subdivision (f) extension of the statute of limitations was also alleged. Appellant pled not guilty. (CT 1:40, 1:62, 1:70-72, 1:74; RT 2:605)

During trial, the prosecution made a sidebar reference to appellant's "rap sheet" audible to some courtroom spectators; appellant had no prior convictions. The court denied counsel's motion for mistrial. (RT 3:1366)

Appellant was found guilty as charged. (CT 1:131-133; RT 4:1802-1803) Appellant was sentenced to the midterm of 12 years, credit for 157 days precommitment confinement, including 20 days conduct credit. (CT 1:194-195; Supp. CT 1:1, 1:3-4; RT 4:2102-2104, 4:2117-2118, 4:2135-2140)

This appeal from a final judgment of conviction is timely. (CT 1:197)

Tragodia 2: Statement of the Case

STATEMENT OF THE CASE

An amended information charged appellant with 101 felonies:kidnaping (counts 1 and 32, Pen. Code § 207(a)); rape in concert (counts 2, 4, 6, 7, 9, 12, 14, 16, 18, 20, 22, 24, 26, 28, 30, 31, 33, 34, 35, 36, 37, 38, 39, 40, 41, 42, 43, 44, 45, 46, 47, 48, 49, 50, 51, 52, 54, 56, 58, 60, 62, 64, 66, 72, 73, 74, 76, 77,. 78, 84, 86, 88, 90, 92, 94, 96, 98, 100, 101, Pen. Code § 264.1); oral copulation in concert (counts 3, 5, 8, 10, 11, 13, 15, 19, 21, 23, 25, 27, 29, 53, 55, 57, 59, 61, 63, 65, 67, 68, 69, 70, 83, 85, 87, 89, 91, 93, 95, 97, 99, Penal Code § 288a(d)); sodomy in concert (counts 71, 80, 81, 82, Pen. Code § 286(d)); anal/genital penetration by foreign object (count 79, Pen. Code § 289(a)).[1] Penal Code section 667.8, subdivision (a) [kidnaping for purposes of committing a sex offense], section 12022 [armed with a handgun], 12022.3, subdivisions (a) and (b) [armed with, and used, a firearm], and section 667.6, subdivision (d) [multiple victims] and California Rules of Court rule 4.421 sentencing allegations[2] were made as to all counts except counts 1 and 32. Section 12022, subdivision (a)(1) allegations were made as to those counts. Appellant pled not guilty. (CT 2:400-404, 5:992-1126, 5:1129)

During trial, the court admonished the prosecutor to refrain from crying and/or openly comforting State witnesses in front of the jury. (RT 3:1281-1282)

During deliberations, the jury requested readback of Faylinn's testimony regarding when "B tells Defendant to rape her or he will shoot him about a prior trial & testimony." (CT 5:1198, 5:1202, 5:1207; RT 8:4801-4803)

Appellant was found guilty as charged on all counts except count 79; the section 667.6, subdivision (d), section 667.8, subdivision (a), and the section 12022, subdivision (a)(1) allegations were found true as charged. The section 12022.3, subdivisions (a) and (b) allegation were found true as to counts 40, 41, 42, 43, 44, 45, 46, 47, 48, 49, 50, 51, 52, 54, 56, 68, 60, 62, 64, 66, 72, 73, 74, and 75. (CT 6:1238-1339, 6:1342-1396, 7:1397-1441; RT 9:5102-5206)

Appellant was sentenced to a total of 862 years: counts 1 and 32 - the midterm of 5 years, plus one year for the section 12022, subdivision (a)(1) allegation, stayed pursuant to section 654; counts 2, 3, 4, 5, 6, 7, 8, 9, 10, 11,

---

1 Callista was the named victim in counts 1 through 31, Faylinn named in counts 32 through 101. (CT 5:1026-1123)

2 The rule 4.421 allegations were that the crimes involved great violence, great bodily harm/threat of great bodily harm or other acts disclosing a high degree of cruelty, that appellant was armed with a handgun during the crimes, that the victims were particularly vulnerable, that the crimes demonstrated planning or professionalism, that appellant was on probation at the time, and performed unsatisfactorily on probation. (CT 5:1123-1124)

12, 13, 14, 15, 16, 17, 18, 19, 20, 21, 22, 23, 24, 25, 26, 27, 28, 29, 30, 31, 34, 35, 36, 37, 38, 39, 53, 55, 57, 59, 61, 63, 65, 67, 68, 69, 70, 71, 76, 77, 78, 79, 81, 82, 83, 84, 85, 86, 87, 88, 89, 90, 91, 92, 93, 94, 95, 96,. 97, 98, 99, 100, and 101 - the midterm of 7 years, plus one year for the section 12022, subdivision (a)(1) allegation, run consecutively; count 33 - the midterm of 7 years, plus one year for the section 12022, subdivision (a)(1), and three years for the section 667.8, subdivision (a) allegation, run consecutively; and counts 40, 41, 42, 43, 44, 45, 46, 47, 48, 49, 50, 51, 52[3], 54, 56, 58, 60, 62, 64, 66, 72, 73, 74, and 75 - the midterm of 7 years, plus four years for the section 12022.3, subdivision (a) allegation, run consecutively. Three year terms for the section 667.8, subdivision (a) allegations on counts 2 through 32, 34 through 78, and 80 through 101 were stayed. Appellant was credited with 2,277 days precomittment confinement, including 759 days conduct credit. (CT 7:1534-1571; RT 9:5407-5431)

    This appeal from a final judgment of conviction is timely. (CT 7:1578)

---

[3]   The section 12022, subdivision (a)(1) allegations were stayed on counts 52, 54, 56, 68, 60, 62, 64, 66.

STATEMENT OF THE CASE

An amended information was filed charging appellant with assault to commit rape (count , Pen. Code § 220), forcible oral copulation (counts 2 and 3, Pen. Code § 288a(c)(2)), penetration by a foreign object (count 4, Pen. Code § 289(a)), assault on a peace officer (count 5, Pen. Code § 245(c) and false imprisonment by violence (count 6, Pen. Code § 236). A Penal Code section 12022, subdivision (b)(1) enhancement was alleged as to count 6; sections 1170.12, subdivisions (a) through (d), 667, subdivision (a)(1), and 667.5, subdivision (b) prior convictions were alleged as to all counts. A section 667.71 prior sex offenses allegation was alleged as to counts 3 and 4, and a section 667.61, subdivision (b) tying and binding allegation made as to counts 2, 3, and 4.[1] Appellant pled not guilty. (CT 1:59-60, 1:82-88, 1:13)

On June 21, 1999, appellant was found guilty of counts 1, 2, 3, 4 and 6 as charged. (CT 1:89-91, 1:193) On August 6, 1999, appellant was sentenced to a total of 225 years to life, credit for 341 days precommitment credit, including 44 days conduct credit. (CT 1:107-110) On October 27, 2006, in *Scott v. Lamarque*, Case No. CV 03-2003-FST(APN), appellant's petition for writ of habeas corpus was granted, and his conviction reversed, pursuant to the magistrate's finding under *Gibson v. Ortiz* (9th Cir. 2004) 387 F.3d 812, that appellant's jury had been improperly instructed as to the prior sex offense evidence. (CT 1:112-130)

Appellant was retried. The court denied appellant's pretrial motion to exclude preliminary hearing testimony. (CT 1: 169-177; RT 2:308-309) Appellant's motion to exclude prior offense evidence was also denied. (RT 2:309-311)

Appellant was found guilty as charged; in a bifurcated proceeding, the priors were found true as alleged. (CT 2:278B-287, 2:289-295; RT 3:2102-2106, 3:2133-2139) Appellant's motions for new trial were denied. (CT 2:398; RT 3:2403) Appellant was sentenced to a total of 278 years, plus 4 life terms: count 1 – 25 years to life, plus 2 years for the prior prison term and 5 years for the serious prior, run consecutive; count 2 – 75 years to life, plus 7 years for prior prison term and prior conviction allegations, run consecutive; count 3 – 75 years to life, plus 7 years for prior prison term and prior conviction allegations, run consecutively; count 4 – 75 years to life, plus 7 years for the prior allegations, run consecutive; count 6 – years, plus 7 years for the prior allegations, stayed pursuant to section 654. Appellant was credited with 3,340 days precommitment confinement. (CT 2:397-401; RT 3:2405-2410)

---

1   The prior convictions stemmed from appellant's Case No. A660563. (CT 1:86)

This appeal from a final judgment of conviction is timely. (CT 402)

STATEMENT OF THE CASE

An information was filed charging appellant with forcible child molestation (counts 1, 2, 3, 4, 5, 6, 7, 8, 9, and 10, Pen. Code § 288(b)(1))and child molestation (counts 11, 12, 13, and 14, Pen. Code § 288(a)).[1] A Penal Code section 667.61, subdivision (b) multiple victim allegation was made as to all counts. Counts 1 through 3 were stricken. Appellant pled not guilty. (CT 40-55, 57-58)

Pre-trial, appellant moved to suppress his statement to police as involuntary. The court denied the motion. (CT ; RT 1:25)

Appellant was found guilty of counts 4 through 14 as charged; the multiple victim allegation was found true. (CT 129-143; RT 2:358-364) Appellant was sentenced to a total of 165 years to life: 15 years to life on each of the eleven counts of conviction, each count to run consecutively. Appellant was credited with 219 days actual precommitment confinement. (CT 161-168; RT 2:369-370)

This appeal from a final judgment of conviction is timely. (CT 169)

---

[1] Count 1 alleged a violation occurring between March 1, 1997 and March 31, 1997 against Phillida; count 2 alleged a violation occurring on December 31, 1997 against Phillida; count 3 alleged a violation occurring on March 4, 1998 against Phillida; count 4 alleged a violation occurring between January 1, 1999 and March 3, 2000 against Phillida; counts 5, 6, 7, 8, and 9 alleged a violation occurring between January 1, 1999 and August 6, 2001 against Paloma; count 10 alleged a violation occurring between October 25, 1999 and October 24, 2001 against Zerlinda; and counts 11, 12, 13 and 14 alleged a violation occurring between May 16, 2003 and May 16, 2007 against Xalba. (RT 2:137-138)

Tragodia 2: Statement of the Case

STATEMENT OF THE CASE

An amended information charged appellant with fifteen counts of residential burglary (counts 1, 5, 10, 15, 17, 24, 27, 31, 39, 48, 52, 54, 59, 61, and 63, Pen. Code § 459), twelve counts of forcible oral copulation (counts 2, 3, 7, 18, 33, 36, 37, 40, 42, 44, 55, and 58, Pen. Code § 288a(c)(2)), twenty-nine counts of rape (counts 4, 8, 9, 11, 12, 13, 14, 19, 20, 21, 22, 23, 25, 25, 29, 30, 32, 34, 35, 38, 43, 45, 46, 47, 49, 50, 51, 56, and 57, Pen. Code § 261(a)(2)), five counts of assault with intent to commit a sex offense (counts 6, 53, 60, 62, and 64, Pen. Code § 220), one count of forcible sodomy (count 16, Pen. Code § 286(c)(2)), and two counts of sexual penetration by foreign object (counts 28 and 41, Pen. Code § 289(a)(1)); Penal Code section 667.61, subdivisions (d)(4) sex offense committed during burglary, burglary commited with intent to commit sex offense and (e)(5) multiple victim allegations were made as to counts 2, 3, 4, 7, 8, 9, 11, 12, 13, 14, 16, 18, 19, 20, 21, 22, 23, 25, 26, 28, 29, 30, 32, 33, 34, 35, 36, 37, 38, 40, 41, 42, 43, 44, 45, 46, 47, 49, 50, 51, 55, 56, 57, and 58; one prior strike under section 1170.12, subdivisions (a) through (d) and two section 667, subdivision (a)(1) prior allegations were made as to all counts. Appellant pled not guilty.[1] (CT 958-1013; RT A-1, D-3, 2077)

Pretrial, the court denied two defense requests to appoint an expert for purposes of presenting expert testimony on the phenomenon of false confessions, finding the evidence was inadmissible under *People v. Kelly* (1976) 17 Cal.3d 24, inadmissible as expert testimony, irrelevant to the facts of appellant's case, and inadmissible pursuant to Evidence Code section 352.[2] (CT 375-410, 412, 483-553; RT C-1, 385-395, 402-503, 834-835; Ex Parte Motion RT 1-7) The court denied a defense request for discovery of DNA evidence relating to uncharged incidents, finding such evidence inherently irrelevant. (CT 648-683; RT C-9-C-12, 69-75) The court granted the State's motion to exclude evidence of third party culpability. (CT 341-345, 714-738; RT 699-708) Pursuant to *People v. Smith* (2003) 107 Cal.App.4th 646, the court ruled evidence of mixed source sample testing would be admitted, admissible under the third prong of *People v. Kelly*, supra, 17 Cal.3d 24, and under a separate admissibility challenge based on *People v. Pizarro* (2003) 110 Cal.App.4th 530. (CT 739-788,

---

1 Counts 42 and 44 were later dismissed under sections 1385 and 1118.1. (CT 951, 953, 956; RT 1882-1883, 1963)

2 The court denied a related motion to suppress the confession under *Miranda v. Arizona* (1966) 384 U.S. 436 . (CT 554- 638; RT 663-699)

804-808; RT 37-43, 47-58, 61-69, 76-142, 151-196, 200-260, 268-301, 304-338)

During deliberations, the jury requested readback of "Jane Doe #13 - sheet evidence, Krisovic - Glove/blood testimony. Det. Kriscovic's ref: on Blanket/Rug, the scientists DNA evidence. Results from Car - police reports. Testimonies from Tarley & Burns who transported Rathbun from Oxnard. Charts 20 & 20B. Jane Doe #4 testimony on feeces & liquid in center." The requested readback was provided. (CT 1015, 1023; RT 2282-2283, 2285-2293, 2306-2314) A second request was made for "evidence that ties fingerprints into Exhibit 20#B." The court responded, "No fingerprint evidence was introduced into evidence in this case." (CT 1016, 1018-1019, 1023; RT 2283-2285) A third request stated, "Count #2 Need to clarify on multiple victims 667.61(e)(5)." (CT 1021; RT 2317-2320, 2322-2323)

Following the appropriate advisements and waivers, appellant waived his right to jury trial on the prior allegations, and the court found the prior true. (CT 1018; RT 2277, 2371)

Appellant was found guilty as charged on counts 1, 2, 3, 4, 5, 6, 7, 8, 9, 10, 11, 12, 13, 14, 15, 16, 17, 18, 19, 20, 21, 22, 23, 27, 28, 29, 30, 31, 32, 33, 34, 35, 36, 37, 38, 39, 40, 41, 43, 45, 46, 47, 48, 49, 50, 51, 52, 53, 54, 55, 56, 57, 58, 59, 60, 61, 62, 63, and 64, and all special section 667.61, subdivisions (d)(4) and (e)(5) allegations found true; he was acquitted on counts 24, 25, and 26. (CT 1128-1227; RT 2326-2361) The court overruled counsel's objection and request for jury trial pursuant to *Blakely v. Washington* (2004) 542 U.S. 296, and sentenced appellant to a total of 1,040 years, plus ten life terms:

count 1 - one-third the midterm of four years, doubled as a second strike, run consecutively;
count 2 - fifty years to life, pursuant to section 667.61, subdivision (d)(4);
count 3 - the upper term of 8 years, doubled as a second strike, run consecutively;
count 4 - the upper term of 8 years, doubled as a second strike, run consecutively;
count 5 - one-third the midterm of four years, doubled as a second strike, run consecutively;
count 6 - the upper term of 6 years, doubled as a second strike;
count 7 - fifty years to life, pursuant to section 667.61, subdivision (d)(4);
count 8 - the upper term of 8 years, doubled as a second strike, run consecutively;
count 9 - the upper term of 8 years, doubled as a second strike, run consecutively;

Tragodia 2: Statement of the Case

count 10 - one-third the midterm of four years, doubled as a second strike, run consecutively;

count 11 - fifty years to life, pursuant to section 667.61, subdivision (d)(4);

count 12 - the upper term of 8 years, doubled as a second strike, run consecutively;

count 13 - the upper term of 8 years, doubled as a second strike, run consecutively;

count 14 - the upper term of 8 years, doubled as a second strike, run consecutively;

count 15 - one-third the midterm of four years, doubled as a second strike, run consecutively;

count 16 - fifty years to life, pursuant to section 667.61, subdivision (d)(4);

count 17 - one-third the midterm of four years, doubled as a second strike, run consecutively;

count 18 - fifty years to life, pursuant to section 667.61, subdivision (d)(4);

count 19 - the upper term of 8 years, doubled as a second strike, run consecutively;

count 20 - the upper term of 8 years, doubled as a second strike, run consecutively;

count 21 - the upper term of 8 years, doubled as a second strike, run consecutively;

count 22 - the upper term of 8 years, doubled as a second strike, run consecutively;

count 23 - the upper term of 8 years, doubled as a second strike, run consecutively;

count 27 - one-third the midterm of four years, doubled as a second strike, run consecutively;

count 28 - fifty years to life, pursuant to section 667.61, subdivision (d)(4);

count 29 - the upper term of 8 years, doubled as a second strike, run consecutively;

count 30 - the upper term of 8 years, doubled as a second strike, run consecutively;

count 31 - one-third the midterm of four years, doubled as a second strike, run consecutively;

count 32 - fifty years to life, pursuant to section 667.61, subdivision (d)(4);

count 33 - the upper term of 8 years, doubled as a second strike, run consecutively;

count 34 - the upper term of 8 years, doubled as a second strike, run consecutively;
count 35 - the upper term of 8 years, doubled as a second strike, run consecutively;
count 36 - the upper term of 8 years, doubled as a second strike, run consecutively;
count 37 - the upper term of 8 years, doubled as a second strike, run consecutively;
count 38 - the upper term of 8 years, doubled as a second strike, run consecutively;
count 39 - one-third the midterm of four years, doubled as a second strike, run consecutively;
count 40 - fifty years to life, pursuant to section 667.61, subdivision (d)(4);
count 41 - the upper term of 8 years, doubled as a second strike, run consecutively;
count 43 - the upper term of 8 years, doubled as a second strike, run consecutively;
count 45 - the upper term of 8 years, doubled as a second strike, run consecutively;
count 46 - the upper term of 8 years, doubled as a second strike, run consecutively;
count 47 - the upper term of 8 years, doubled as a second strike, run consecutively;
count 48 - one-third the midterm of four years, doubled as a second strike, run consecutively;
count 49 - fifty years to life, pursuant to section 667.61, subdivision (d)(4);
count 50 - the upper term of 8 years, doubled as a second strike, run consecutively;
count 51 - the upper term of 8 years, doubled as a second strike, run consecutively;
count 52 - one-third the midterm of four years, doubled as a second strike, run consecutively;
count 53 - one-third the midterm of four years, doubled as a second strike, run consecutively;
count 54 - one-third the midterm of four years, doubled as a second strike, run consecutively;
count 55 - fifty years to life, pursuant to section 667.61, subdivision (d)(4);

Tragodía 2: Statement of the Case

count 56 - the upper term of 8 years, doubled as a second strike, run consecutively;

count 57 - the upper term of 8 years, doubled as a second strike, run consecutively;

count 58 - the upper term of 8 years, doubled as a second strike, run consecutively;

count 59 - one-third the midterm of four years, doubled as a second strike, run consecutively;

count 60 - one-third the midterm of four years, doubled as a second strike, run consecutively;

count 61 - one-third the midterm of four years, doubled as a second strike, run consecutively;

count 62 - one-third the midterm of four years, doubled as a second strike, run consecutively;

count 63 - one-third the midterm of four years, doubled as a second strike, consecutive; and

count 64 - one-third the midterm of four years, doubled as a second strike, run consecutively.

Appellant was credited with 1,038 days precomittment confinement, including 346 days conduct credit. (CT 1377- 1398; RT 2387-2401)

This appeal from a final judgment of conviction is timely. (CT 1399-1402)

STATEMENT OF THE CASE

An information was filed charging appellant with residential burglary (count 1, Pen. Code § 459), rape (counts 2 and 4, Pen. Code § 261(a)(2)), forcible sodomy (count 3, Pen. Code § 286(c)(2)), and sexual penetration by foreign object (count 5, Pen. Code § 289(a)(1)); a Penal Code section 667.61, subdivisions (a), (b), (d) and (e) burglary, tying and binding and weapon use allegations were made as to counts 2 through 5. A Penal Code section 12022.53, subdivision (b) weapon use allegation was made as to counts 2 through 5. Aggravated sentencing factors were alleged under California Rules of Court, rule 4.421 that the crime involved great bodily injury, weapon use, a vulnerable victim, planning/sophistication, and abuse of a position of trust. Appellant pled not guilty. (CT 1:99-107, 1:111)

Following the appropriate advisements, appellant waived his right to a jury trial. (CT 1:233; RT 2:302-303) The court found appellant guilty as charged, and found the section 667.61 tying and binding and firearm allegations true. The court found weapon use, great bodily injury, victim vulnerability, planning/sophistication, and abuse of a position of trust as factors in aggravation. (CT 3:413-415; RT 5:4204-4206, 5:4502-4503)

Appellant was sentenced to a total of 53 years to life: count 1 - the midterm of 4 years, stayed pursuant to section 654; count 2 - 25 years to life, pursuant to section 667.61, subdivisions (a),(d) and (e); count 3 - the midterm of 6 years, plus 10 years pursuant to section 12022.53, subdivision (b), run consecutive; count 4 - the midterm of 6 years, run consecutive; and count 5 - the midterm of 6 years, run consecutive. Appellant was credited with 1255 days precommitment confinement, including 161 days conduct credit. (CT 3:435-438, 3:452-458; RT 5:4516-4519, 5:4521-4522-4800)

This appeal from a final judgment of conviction is timely. (CT 3: 461)

Tragodia 2: Statement of the Case

STATEMENT OF THE CASE

An amended information charged appellant with corporal injury to spouse (count 1, Pen. Code § 273.5(a)), aggravated mayhem (count 2, Pen. Code § 205), torture (count 3, Pen. Code section 206), and forcible sodomy (counts 4, 5, 6, and 7, Pen. Code § 286(c)(2)); a Penal Code section 12022.7, subdivision (e) great bodily injury resulting from domestic violence allegation was made as to count 1.[1] Appellant pled not guilty. (CT 92-98, 100, 110)

Appellant was found guilty as charged, and the section 12022.7 allegation found true. (CT 173-180; RT 1635-1639, 1641-1642) Appellant was sentenced to life, plus 32 years in state prison: count 3 - life; count 4 - the upper term of 8 years, run consecutive; count 5 - the upper term of 8 years, run consecutive; count 6 - the upper term of 8 years, run consecutive; and count 7 - the upper term of 8 years, run consecutive. Appellant was credited with 188 days precommitment confinement, including 24 days conduct credit. (CT 195-201; RT 1661-1664)

This appeal from a final judgment of conviction is timely. (CT 202)

---

[1] Count 1 was subsequently dismissed on the prosecution's motion; count 2 was dismissed pursuant to Penal Code section 1385. (CT 110, 119; RT 902-903)

Tragodia 2: Statement of the Case

STATEMENT OF THE CASE

An amended information was filed charging appellant with burglary (counts 1, 19, 25 and 27 Pen. Code § 459), sexual penetration by foreign object (counts 2, 9, 10, 22 and 29, Pen. Code § 289(a)(1)), attempted murder (count 3, Pen. Code §§ 664/187) rape (counts 4, 5, 6, 7, 8, 11, 16, 17, 21 and 28), forcible sodomy (counts 12, 15 and 23, Pen. Code § 286(c)(2)), forcible oral copulation (counts 13, 14 and 20, Pen. Code § 288a(c)(2)), false imprisonment by violence (count 18, Pen. Code § 236), robbery (count 23, Pen. Code § 211), and assault to commit a felony during the commission of a first degree burglary (count 26, Pen. Code § 220(b)). A Penal Code section 12022, subdivision (b)(1) firearm allegation and a section 12022.3, subdivisions (a) and (b) knife use allegation were made as to counts 2, 4, 5, 6, 7, 8, 9, 10, 11, 12, 13, 14, 15, 16, 17, 20, 21, 22, 23, 28 and 29. A Penal Code section 667.61, subdivisions (a)(b)(d) weapon use allegation was made as to count 2, subdivisions (a)(b)(d)(e) multiple victim, commission during commission of a residential burglary, and deadly weapon use allegations made as to counts 2, 4, 5, 6, 7, 8, 9, 10, 11, 12, 13, 14, 15, 16 17, 20, 21, 22, 23, 28 and 29.[1] Appellant pled not guilty. (CT 2:367-399)

During deliberations, the jury asked for readback of Addie's testimony. After a break, the jury sent a note indicating further readback was unnecessary. The jury also requested the knife and jewelry. (CT 4:771-773, 4:806-807)

Appellant was found guilty as charged on counts 1, 2, 4, 5, 6, 7, 8, 9, 10, 11 12, 13, 14, 15, 16, 17, 18, 19, 20, 21, 22, 23, 25, 26, 27, 28 and 29. The jury found the Penal Code section 667.5, subdivision (c) [third party present] allegation true on counts 1, 19, 25, 27. The allegation that the offense was committed during a residential burglary with the intent to commit a sex offense was found true as to counts 2, 4, 5, 6, 7, 8, 9, 10, 11, 12, 13, 14, 15, 16, 17, 20, 21, 22, 23, 28 and 29. The multiple victim allegation was found true as to counts 2, 4, 5, 6, 7, 8, 9, 10, 11, 12, 13, 14, 15, 16, 17, 20, 21, 22, 23, 28 and 29. The knife allegations were found not true as to count 1, and true as to counts 2, 4, 5, 6, 7, 8, 9, 10, 11, 12, 13, 14, 15, 16, 17, 18, 19, 20, 21, 22, 23, 28 and 29. Appellant was acquitted of counts 3 and 24, and found guilty of larceny as a lesser offense to count 24. (CT 4:774-803, 4:807-829)

---

1   Counts 1, 2, 3, 4, 5, 6, 7, 8, 9, 10, 11, 12, 13, 14, 15, 16, and 17 alleged a violation occurring on January 2, 2007, naming Ban as the victim; counts 19, 20, 21, 22, 23, 24, 28 and 29 alleged a violation occurring on March 29, 2007, naming Paige as the victim; counts 25 and 26 alleged a violation occurring on June 26, 2007, naming Chanthara as victim; and count 27 alleged a violation occurring on September 10, 2007, naming Nissa as victim. (CT 2:371-395)

Appellant was sentenced to a total of 648 years, plus 22 life terms: the midterm of 4 years on count 1; one-third the midterm of 8 months on count 18, plus one-third the midterm of 4 months for the knife use, run consecutively; the midterm of 4 years on count 19; life on count 26; 29 years to life on counts 2, 4, 5, 6, 7, 8, 9, 10, 11, 12, 13, 14, 15, 16, 17 (25 years to life pursuant to section 667.61, subdivisions (a)(b)(e) plus the midterm of 4 years for the knife use); 35 years to life on counts 20, 21, 22, 23, 28 and 29. Counts 1, 19 and 25 were stayed pursuant to section 654; all counts were run consecutively. Appellant was credited with 622 days precommitment confinement, including 81 days conduct credit. (CT 4:901-923)

This appeal from a final judgment of conviction is timely. (CT 4:924)

Tragodia 2: Statement of the Case

STATEMENT OF THE CASE

An amended information was filed charging appellant with aggravated sexual assault of a child/oral copulation (count 1, Pen. Code § 269(a)(4)), child molestation (counts 2 through 7, Pen. Code § 288(a)(1)); a Penal Code section 1203.066, subdivision (a)(9) [use of obscene matter] allegation was made as to count 4, a subdivision (a)(8) allegation [substantial sexual conduct] made as to counts 2, 3, 4, 5 and 6, and a subdivision (a)(3) [making friends with victim] allegation made as to counts 2, 3, 4, 5, 6 and 7.[1] Appellant pled not guilty. (CT 91, 94-103, 131-132, 135-136; RT 2:485-486)

Appellant was found guilty as charged. (CT 210-217; RT 3:621-623) Appellant was sentenced to a total of 15 years to life: count 1 - 15 years to life; count 2 - the low term of 3 years; count 3 - the low term of 3 years; count 4 - the low term of 3 years; count 5 - the low term of 3 years; count 6 - the low term of 3 years; counts 2, 3, 4, 5, and 6 were run concurrently with count 1. Appellant was credited with 450 days precommitment confinement, including 95 days conduct credit. (CT 232-239; RT 3:636-638)

This appeal from a final judgment of conviction is timely. (CT 231)

---

1   All section 1203.066, subdivision (a) allegations were later stricken on the People's motion, and count 7 was dismissed. (CT 127, 132; RT 1:56-57) The dates alleged were amended to conform to proof, over defense objection. (RT 2:484-485)

STATEMENT OF THE CASE[1]

Following reversal of his 115 years-to life sentence;[2] appellant was remanded for resentencing on his convictions of rape (count 1, Pen. Code § 261(a)(2)), penetration by a foreign object (counts 2 and 3, Pen. Code § 289(a)(1)), and sexual battery/masturbation (count 4, Pen. Code § 243.4(c)). Three prior convictions were found true pursuant to Penal Code sections 667, subdivision (a), 1170.12, subdivisions (a) through (d), and 667, subdivisions (b) through (i). (CT 1-16; RT 2) At resentencing, appellant argued imposition of consecutive terms constituted cruel and unusual punishment, violated federal and state due process and equal protection guarantees, and ran afoul of the California Supreme Court's opinion in *People v. Jones* (2001) 25 Cal.4th 98. (CT 18-33; RT 8-10) The trial court rejected the cruel and unusual punishment argument based on appellant's record,[3] and distinguished *Jones* as predicated on a section 667.6 [sic]" analysis, rather than the section 667.6, subdivision (d) determination made in appellant's case. (RT 11)

The court then resentenced appellant to a total of 90 years to life: count 1 - 30 years to life, 25 years to life for the strike term, plus 5 years for the section 667, subdivision (a) finding, to run consecutive; count 2 - 30 years to life, the three strike term plus the five year prior, also run consecutive; count 3 - 30 years to life, the three strike term plus five year prior, run consecutive; count 4 - the upper term of 4 years to run concurrent. Appellant was given credit for 954 days precommittment confinement, including 36 days conduct credit. (CT 41-46; RT 11-12)

This appeal from a final judgment of conviction is timely. (CT 47-48)

---

1   As this is an appeal from appellant's resentencing, there is no need for a Statement of Facts; appellant would ask the Court to take judicial notice of the facts as set forth in Case No. B147813. (Evid. Code § 453(d); *People v. Hill* (1998) 17 Cal.4th 800, 847, fn. 9.)

2   This Court reversed appellant's sentence for the trial court's application of a Three Strikes finding to a count in which no strikes allegation had been made. (CT 15-16; RT 7) In remanding, the Court indicated appellant could raise his consecutive sentencing and cruel and unusual punishment claims in the trial court. (CT 15; RT 3, 7, 10)

3   In 1977, in Case No. A330628, appellant was convicted of robbery and second degree murder; that conviction was reversed, and appellant pled to second degree murder in 1979, and was sentenced to 5 years to life. He was paroled in 1981. Parole was violated in 1982, and appellant convicted, in Case No. A378633, of robbery and rape in concert. Appellant was sentenced to 5 years. In 1985, in Case No. A767632, appellant was convicted of attempted burglary, and sentenced to 18 months; in 1987, in Case No. 87M34256, appellant was convicted of misdemeanor child abuse, and sentenced to 24 days in jail. In 1988, in Case No. A980690, appellant was convicted of first degree robbery and residential burglary, and sentenced to 19 years; appellant was on parole at the time of the charges in this case. (Supp. CT pp. 4-5, 10.)

Tragodia 2: Statement of the Case

STATEMENT OF THE CASE

An amended information charged appellant with forcible oral copulation in concert (count 1, Pen. Code § 288a(d)), rape in concert (count 2, Pen. Code § 264.1), forcible sodomy in concert (count 3, Pen. Code § 286(d)), kidnaping for robbery (count 4, Pen. Code § 209(b)(1)), robbery (counts 5 and 6, Pen. Code § 211), forcible oral copulation (count 7, Pen. Code § 288a(c)(2)), rape (count 8, Pen. Code § 261(a)(2)), forcible sodomy (count 9, Pen. Code § 286(c)(2)); a Penal Code section 667.61, subdivision (b) allegation was made as to all counts.[1] Appellant pled not guilty. (CT 81-93, 126-127, 358; RT C-1)

The prosecution's motion to admit pursuant to Evidence Code section 1108 was granted over defense objection. (CT 313-316; RT 2-5)

Appellant moved to join four other cases which had been consolidated for purposes of a combined *Kelly*[2] hearing on the general acceptance of the specific DNA typing process employed in appellant's case; the court denied the motion. (CT 143-147, 149-207, 237; RT D2-D6) Appellant's own motion for a Kelly hearing on prongs 1 and 2 was denied; following an Evidence Code section 402 hearing, the court found prong 3 had been established. (CT 285-292, 309, 328-329, 369-370; RT F-7, F-42) After a Wheeler motion was granted as to the first venire, but before the second was empaneled, the court permitted the prosecution to bring in new DNA calculations based on a different population database as potential rebuttal testimony. The court later allowed the evidence as part of the case-in-chief. (RT 171-172, 251, 377-381, 399-409)

Appellant was found guilty as charged; the kidnaping allegations on counts 1, 2, 3, 7, 8, and 9 were found true. (CT 461A-461H, 461J, 462-466; RT 1871-1877) Appellant was sentenced to a total of 39 years to life; count 1 - the midterm of 7 years; count 2 - the midterm of 7 years; count 3 - the midterm of 7 years; count 4 - life; count 5 - the midterm of 3 years; count 7 - the midterm of 6 years; count 8 - the midterm of 6 years; count 9 - 15 years to life. All terms were run consecutive under section 667.6, subdivision (d); count 6 was stayed pursuant to Penal Code section 654. (CT 486-489, 491-493; RT 1898-1901) Appellant was credited with 1,129 days precommittment confinement, including 147 days conduct credit. (CT 489; RT 1903)

This appeal from a final judgment of conviction is timely. (CT 495-496)

---

1   The co-perpetrator was convicted before appellant's trial. (CT 113-114, 357, 359)

2   (*People v. Kelly* (1976) 17 Cal.3d 24.)

Tragodia 2: Statement of the Case

STATEMENT OF THE CASE

An information was filed charging appellant with meeting a minor for lewd purposes (count 1, Pen. Code § 288.3 (b)). Appellant pled not guilty. (CT 5-6, 8)

Appellant was found guilty as charged. (CT 109-111; RT 2:294-296) Appellant was sentenced to 5 years formal probation, conditions of which include serving 198 days in county jail, credit for 198 days precomittment confinement, and a series of travel/residency, internet/communication and associational restrictions. Appellant was required to register as a sex offender pursuant to Penal Code sections 290 and 3003.5. (CT 136-139; RT 2:316-320)

This appeal from a final judgment of conviction is timely. (CT 140)

STATEMENT OF THE CASE

On October 17, 2007, this Court issued an opinion in Case No. B186713, affirming the convictions and remanding for resentencing pursuant to *People v. Sandoval* (2007) 41 Cal.4th 825. (CT 4-32) The remittitur was issued on December 21, 2007. (CT 3)

On December 2, 2008, the trial court resentenced appellant to a total of 22 years: count 10 – the midterm of 6 years; count 11 – one-third the midterm of 2 years, run consecutively; count 12- one-third the midterm of 2 years, run consecutively; count 13 – the midterm of 6 years, run consecutively; and count 14 – the midterm of 6 years, run consecutively. Appellant was credited with 1,453 days credit. (CT 91-96; RT 16-20/300)

This appeal is timely. (CT 20-24)

STATEMENT OF THE CASE

An amended information charged appellant with sexual penetration by foreign object (count 1, Pen. Code § 289(a)(1)), child abuse (count 2, Pen. Code § 273a(a)) and corporal injury to child (count 3, Pen. Code § 273d(a)); Penal Code section 12022.7, subdivisions (a) and (d) great bodily injury enhancements were alleged as to all counts. Great violence, victim vulnerability, and abuse of a position of trust were alleged as factors in aggravation under California Rules of Court, rule 4.421(a)(1)(3)(11). Appellant pled not guilty. (CT 1:151, 1:158, 2:414-417; RT 2:E-39)

Appellant was found guilty as charged on counts 1 and 3; the great bodily injury enhancement was found not true.[1] (CT 4:732-738; RT 13:3607-3608) The defense motion for new trial was denied. (RT 14:3908) Appellant was sentenced to a total of 8 years in state prison: count 1 - the upper term of 8 years; and count 3 - the upper term of 6 years, stayed pursuant to Penal Code section 654. Appellant received 59 days credit for precommitment confinement, including 8 days conduct credit. (CT 4:813-817; CT 1/1[2]:1-2; RT 14:3939-3945)

This appeal from a final judgment of conviction is timely. (CT 4:812)

---

[1] Count 2 was dismissed on motion of the prosecution. (CT 4:734, 4:737; RT 14:3939)

[2] The second Clerk's Transcript, date stamped August 12, 2008; to be distinguished from the Clerk's Transcripts date stamped July 3, 2008.

Tragodia 2: Statement of the Case

STATEMENT OF THE CASE

An amended information charged appellant with attempted kidnaping (count 2, Pen. Code §§ 664/207(a)), pimping (counts 3, 7 and 11, Pen. Code § 266h(a)), pandering by procuring (counts 4, 6, 8 and 12, Pen. Code § 266i(a)(1)), attempted pandering by procuring (count 5, Pen. Code §§ 664/266i(a)(1)), false imprisonment by violence (counts 9, 19 and 22, Pen. Code § 236), rape (count 10, Pen. Code § 261(a)(2)), aggravated sexual assault of a child (count 13, Pen. Code § 261(A)(2)), forcible child molestation (count 14, Pen. Code § 288(b)(1)), child molestation (count 15, Pen. Code § 288(a)), aggravated sexual assault of a child/oral copulation (count 16, Pen. Code § 269(a)(4)), forcible oral copulation (count 18, Pen. Code § 288a(c)), and procuring a child to engage in a lewd act (counts 20 and 21, Pen. Code § 266j). A Penal Code section 667.5, subdivision (b) prior prison term was alleged as to count 4.[1] Appellant pled not guilty. (CT 2:302-314)

Over defense objection, the court admitted expert testimony on pimping and prostitution. (RT 1:31-33) Also over objection, one of the victim-witnesses was allowed to testify wearing sunglasses and a scarf. (RT 4:769-770, 4:851-852, 5:903)

Appellant was found guilty as charged on counts 3, 4, 5, 6, 7, 8, 9, 10, 11, 12, 13, 14, 15, 16, 18, 19, 20, 21, and 22. The section 12022, subdivision (b)(1) allegation on count 9 was found true. He was acquitted on count 2; the prior conviction allegation was found not true. (CT 2:459-487; RT Supp.1:1-14, 19-20)

Appellant was sentenced to 54 years to life: count 3 - one-third the midterm of 16 months, run consecutive because the offense was committed at a different time or place, and involved a separate act of violence or threat of violence; count 4 - one-third the midterm of 16 months, run consecutive; count 5 -one-third the midterm of 8 months, run consecutive; count 6 - one-third the midterm of 16 months, run consecutive; count 7 - one-third the midterm of 16 months, run consecutive; count 8 - the midterm of 4 years, stayed pursuant to section 654; count 9 - the midterm of 2 years, plus one year for the section 12022, subdivision (b)(1) allegation, stayed under section 654; count 10 - the midterm of 6 years; count 11 - one-third the midterm of 16 months, run consecutive; count 12 - the midterm of 4 years, stayed under section 654; count 13 - 15

---

[1] Counts 2, 5, and 22 named LaVonda Williams as the victim; counts 3, 4, 9, 19, 10, and 18, named Chantel S.; Shantay R. was named in counts 7, 8, and 20; Keisha H. the victim in counts 11, 12, 13, 14, 15, 16, and 21; and Brandy T. the count 6 victim. (CT 2:302-312)

years to life; count 14 - the midterm of 6 years, stayed under section 654; count 15 - the midterm of 6 years, stayed under section 654; count 16 - 15 years to life, run consecutive; count 18 - the midterm of 6 years, run consecutive under section 667.6, subdivision (d); count 19 - the midterm of 2 years, stayed under section 654; count 20 - one-third the midterm of 24 months, run consecutive; count 21 - one-third the midterm of 24 months, run consecutive; count 22 - one-third the midterm of 8 months, run consecutive. Counsel objected to the court's imposition of the consecutive term under *Blakely v. Washington* (2004) 542 U.S. 296, the separate occasions characterization of the offenses, and to the court's failure to apply section 654 to counts 5 and 22, 3 and 4, 7 and 8, 11 and 12, 13 and 14, and 15 and 16. Appellant was credited with 862 days precommitment confinement, including 112 days conduct credit. (CT 2:515-527; RT Supp.1:65-75)

This appeal from a final judgment of conviction is timely. (CT 2:528)

STATEMENT OF THE CASE

Pursuant to this Court's opinion in *People v. Chan* (2005) 128 Cal. App.4th 408, appellant was remanded to the trial court for resentencing; the court dismissed all lesser included offenses, and imposed consecutive terms on each count of conviction under Penal Code section 1170.12. (CT 1-24, 27-29)

Appellant was sentenced to a total of 256 years state prison, plus ten life terms. Appellant was credited with 626 days precommitment confinement, including 208 days conduct credit. (CT 28-31; RT 2-3)

This appeal from a final judgment of conviction is timely. (CT 32-33)

Tragodia 2: Statement of the Case

STATEMENT OF THE CASE

An amended information charged appellant with three counts of child molestation (Pen. Code § 288(a)); Penal Code sections 667.51, subdivision (a) and 667.6, subdivision (a) prior sex offense allegations were filed as to all counts,[1] as were three prior burglary convictions, which were filed pursuant to Penal Code sections 1170.12, subdivisions (a) through (d) and 667, subdivision (b) through (i). (CT 98-100) Appellant pled not guilty to all counts, and denied the allegations. (CT 102, 116) Count three was later dismissed pursuant to section 1385, as were the sections 667.51, subdivision (a) and 667.6, subdivision (a) allegations. (CT 124, 177; RT 248)

Just prior to the defense case, the court signed an order to have appellant's knife, which had been booked into his jail property, transported to court. (RT 92) The knife was not transported; after appellant's testimony, his attorney faxed the order to the jail. The knife was not delivered. (RT 134, 136)

The court denied the defense request to sanitize appellant's prior burglary and sexual battery convictions for impeachment purposes. (CT 128; RT 94-100) Appellant was found guilty as charged. Appellant waived his right to jury trial on the prior allegations. The court found the Pennsylvania burglary priors true, found they were residential burglaries under California law, and denied the defense request to strike or more under *People v. Superior Court (Romero)* 13 Cal.4th 497. (CT 172-175, 177, 242-243; RT 229-234, 278, 286-297, 302-311, 313-324)

Appellant was sentenced to a total of 26 years to life: 25 years to life on counts one and two, run concurrently, and one-third the midterm of one year for the sexual battery in Case No. NA042578, run consecutively. Appellant was credited with 271 days in Case No. TA061694-01 (including 35 days conduct credit), and 879 days in Case No. NA042578 (including 118 days conduct credit). (CT 37-38, 244-249; RT 324-327)

This appeal from a final judgment of conviction is timely. (CT 250)

---

1   In Case No. NA052458, appellant was charged with one count each of attempted oral copulation of an unconscious person (count 1, Pen. Code §§ 664/288a(f)) and misdemeanor child molestation (count 2, Pen. Code § 647.6(a)). (CT 13-17; RT A-2) The counts concerned separate incidents, none of which were related to the current case, and which were the basis for the section 667.51, subdivision (a) and 667.6, subdivision (a) allegations. Appellant pled to a lesser-related count 3 of sexual battery, and was placed on five years formal probation, the conditions of which included spending one year in county jail, credit for 525 days precommittment confinement. (CT 18-19; RT A-13-A-17, 318-319) After appellant was convicted in the present case, he was found in violation of probation in Case No. NA062858, probation was revoked, and appellant sentenced to one-third the midterm of one year in state prison, run consecutive. (CT 20-36, 177; RT 242-243, 326-327)

STATEMENT OF THE CASE

An information charged appellant with child molestation (counts 1 and 2, Pen. Code § 288(a)); a Penal Code section 667.61, subdivision (b) multiple-victim allegation was alleged as to both counts. Appellant pled not guilty. (CT 80-82, 84)

On December 4, 2002, appellant's *People v. Marsden* (1970) 2 Cal.3d 118 motion to substitute the public defender was denied, as well as his request to obtain private counsel. (CT 91; RT 2-18)

The court granted the prosecution motion to introduce evidence of other sex offenses pursuant to Evidence Code sections 1101, subdivision (b) and 1108. (CT 93-97; RT 306-307, 658-660)

Appellant was convicted as charged; the section 667.61, subdivision (b) allegation was found true. (CT 149-153; RT 1204-1208) Appellant's trial counsel filed a motion to dismiss the One Strike allegation as cruel and unusual punishment; before the motion was heard, private counsel substituted in for trial counsel. New counsel moved for a new trial on a number of grounds, and the court denied the motion. (CT 154-162, 167, 170-187; RT 1801-1804) Appellant was sentenced to a total of 15 years to life: count 1 - 15 years to life; count 2 - 15 years to life. Appellant was credited with 296 days precommitment confinement, including 48 days conduct credit. (CT 187-188, 193-194; RT 1804-1807)

This appeal from a final judgment of conviction is timely. (CT 195)

Tragodia 2: Statement of the Case

STATEMENT OF THE CASE

An amended information charged appellant with four counts of making criminal threats (counts 1, 10, 11 and 17, Pen. Code § 422), thirteen counts of assault with a deadly weapon/by means of force likely to cause great bodily injury (counts 2, 3, 6, 12, 15, 16, 20, 21, 22, 23, 24, 26, 33, Pen. Code § 245(a)(1)), one count of use of a destructive device and explosive to injure/destroy (count 4, Pen. Code § 12303.3), one count of possession of a destructive device near a private habitation and other public place (count 5, Pen. Code § 12303.2), two counts of spouse abuse (counts 7 and 13, Pen. Code § 273.5(a)), one count of aggravated mayhem (count 8, Pen. Code § 205), two counts of discharging a firearm with gross negligence (counts 9 and 19, Pen. Code § 246.3), one count of spousal rape (count 14, Pen. Code § 262(a)(1)), one count of assault with a semiautomatic firearm (count 18, Pen. Code § 245(b)), one count of false imprisonment by violence (count 25, Pen. Code § 236), one count of assault with a stun gun or taser (count 27, Pen. Code § 244.5(b)), one count of sexual penetration by foreign object (count 28, Pen. Code § 289(a)(1)), one count of attempted torture (count 29, Pen. Code §§ 664/206), two counts of child molestation/defendant at least ten years older than victim (counts 30 and 31, Pen. Code § 288(c)(1)), one count of rape (count 32, Pen. Code § 261(a)(2)), three counts of ex-felon in possession of a firearm/two priors (counts 34, 35 and 36, Pen. Code § 12021(a)(1)), one count of possession of a deadly weapon (count 37, Pen. Code § 12020(a)(1)), one count of possession of an assault weapon (count 38, Pen. Code § 12280(b)), two counts of possession of a destructive device (count 39 and 40, Pen. Code § 12303), one count of illegal possession of ammunition (count 41, Pen. Code § 12316(b)(1)), two counts of witness intimidation (counts 42 and 43, Pen. Code § 137), and one count of stalking (count 44, Pen. Code § 646.9(a)). Prior convictions for assault with a deadly weapon and robbery were alleged as to all counts pursuant to Penal Code sections 1170.12, subdivisions (a) through (d); a section 667, subdivision (a)(1) allegation was made as to counts 5, 15, 16, 20, 21, 22, 23, 24, 25, 26, 27, 33, 34, 35, 36, 37, 38, 39, 40, 41, 42, 43 and 44. A section 667.61, subdivision (b) multiple victim allegation was made as to counts 14, 28 and 32. A section 12022, subdivision (a)(1) weapon use allegation was made as to count 17; a section 12022, subdivision (b)(1) weapon use allegation made as to counts 7, 8, 19, 11, 13, 14 and 29, and a section 12022.5, subdivisions (a) and (d) weapon use allegation as to count 18. Appellant pled not guilty, and denied all special allegations. (CT 220-246, 256; RT 48)

It was stipulated at trial that appellant had been previously convicted of a felony, that the Harrington and Richardson shotgun was a sawed-off shotgun, that the Harrington and Richardson sawed-off shotgun and a .357 magnum revolver were recovered from a file cabinet in appellant's home, and that a shotgun barrel, a Garand M-1 rifle, a JC Higgins rifle, a Remington shotgun, a German .98 rifle, a Spain Fabricade Arma rifle, and two canons were recovered from his garage. It was further stipulated that a Marlin rifle, a Remington shotgun, a Bushmaster XM15-E25 rifle, a Carbin Rugar rifle and two SKS Russian rifles were found in a gun safe in the back bedroom closet, a Mossberg shotgun was found in the back bedroom under the bed, and a Ravin Arms semi-automatic handgun and two Smith and Wesson semi-automatic handguns were taken from the living room. It was stipulated bullets, live rounds, weapons paraphernalia, gun powder, and eight additional rifles were recovered throughout the location, that the cannons were destructive devices as statutorily defined, and the Bushmaster XM15-E25 is an assault weapon as statutorily defined. (RT 653-654, 1569-1570)

Following the appropriate advisements and waivers, appellant admitted his prior convictions pursuant to sections 1170.12, subdivision (a) through (d), and 667, subdivision (a)(1). (CT 393-394; RT 2109-2115) During deliberations, the jury requested readback of Doe's testimony on counts 22 and 23; the jury also asked for clarification on the B.B. pump-action rifle with C-02 cartridge charged in the information; the prosecution struck the C-02 allegation. (CT 393-394, 487; RT 2104-2108)

Appellant was found guilty as charged on all counts except count 15; on that count, the jury found him guilty of the lesser included offense of misdemeanor assault.[1] The section 12022, subdivision (b)(1) allegation was found true on counts 7, 8, 10, 11, 13 and 29; the section 12022, subdivision (a) (1) allegation true on count 17; the section 12022.5, subdivision (a) allegation true as to count 18, and the section 667.61, subdivision (b) allegation true as to counts 14 and/or 28, and 32. (CT 348-391, 396-410; RT 2119-2142)

The court denied appellant's request to dismiss the strikes pursuant to section 1385, and to reduce counts 1, 2, 3, 6, 7, 9, 10, 11, 12, 13, 15, 17, 19, 20, 21, 22, 23, 24, 25, 26, 27, 30, 31, 33, 37, 38, 39, 40, 41, and 44 to misdemeanors under section 17, subdivision (b). (CT 411, 421, 442; RT 2402-2403)

---

1   A section 1118.1 motion was granted as to counts 16 and 21. (CT 300; RT 1597-1599, 1802)

Tragodia 2: Statement of the Case

Appellant was sentenced to a total of 1,002 years to life:[2]

count 1 - 25 years to life as a third strike, run consecutive;
count 2 - 25 years to life as a third strike, run consecutive;
count 3 - 25 years to life as a third strike, run consecutive;
count 4 - 25 years to life as a third strike, run consecutive;
count 5 - 25 years to life as a third strike, stayed pursuant to section 654;
count 6 - 25 years to life as a third strike, run consecutive;
count 7 - 25 years to life as a third strike, plus 1 year for the section 12022, subdivision (b)(1) allegation, stayed under section 654;
count 8 - 25 years to life as a third strike, plus 1 year for the section 12022, subdivision (b)(1) allegation, run consecutive;
count 9 - 25 years to life as a third strike, run consecutive;
count 10 - 25 years to life as a third strike, run consecutive, the section 12022, subdivision (b)(1) term stricken;
count 11 - 25 years to life as a third strike, run consecutive, the section 12022, subdivision (b)(1) term stricken;
count 12 - 25 years to life as a third strike, stayed under section 654;
count 13 - 25 years to life as a third strike, plus 1 year for the section 12022, subdivision (b)(1) allegation, run consecutive;
count 14 - 45 years to life as a third strike, run consecutive;
count 15 - 180 days County Jail, run concurrent, credit for time served;
count 17 - 25 years to life as a third strike, plus 1 year for the section 12022, subdivision (a)(1) allegation, run consecutive;
count 18 - 25 years to life as a third strike, plus 4 years for the section 12022.5, subdivision (a) allegation, run consecutive;
count 19 - 25 years to life as a third strike, run consecutive;
count 20 - 25 years to life as a third strike, run consecutive;
count 22 - 25 years to life as a third strike, run consecutive;
count 23 - 25 years to life as a third strike, run consecutive;
count 24 - 25 years to life as a third strike, run consecutive;
count 25 - 25 years to life as a third strike, run consecutive;
count 26 - 25 years to life as a third strike, run consecutive;
count 27 - 25 years to life as a third strike, run consecutive;
count 28 - 45 years to life: 15 years to life tripled as a third strike, run consecutive;

---

2   2 Count 32 was the base count. (CT 442; RT 2418)

count 29 - 25 years to life as a third strike, the section 12022, subdivision (b)(1) term stricken, stayed under section 654;
count 30 - 25 years to life as a third strike, run consecutive;
count 31 - 25 years to life as a third strike, run consecutive;
count 32 - 45 years to life: 15 years to life tripled as a third strike;
count 33 - 25 years to life as a third strike, run consecutive;
count 34 - 25 years to life as a third strike, run consecutive;
count 35 - 25 years to life as a third strike, run consecutive;
count 36 - 25 years to life as a third strike, run consecutive;
count 37 - 25 years to life as a third strike, run consecutive;
count 38 - 25 years to life as a third strike, run consecutive;
count 39 - 25 years to life as a third strike, run consecutive;
count 40 - 25 years to life as a third strike, run consecutive;
count 41 - 25 years to life as a third strike, run consecutive, plus 5 years for the section 667, subdivision (a)(1) allegation;
count 42 - 25 years to life as a third strike, run consecutive, plus 5 years for the section 667, subdivision (a)(1) allegation;
count 43 - 25 years to life as a third strike, run consecutive, plus 5 years for the section 667, subdivision (a)(1) allegation;
count 44 - 25 years to life as a third strike, run consecutive, plus 5 years for the section 667, subdivision (a)(1) allegation.

Appellant was credited with 150 days precommitment confinement, including 20 days conduct credit. (CT 442-463; RT 2418-2427)

This appeal from a final judgment of conviction is timely. (CT 486)

Tragodia 2: Statement of the Case

STATEMENT OF THE CASE

An information was filed charging appellant with pandering by encouraging (Pen. Code § 266i (a)(2)). (CT 13-14) Appellant pled not guilty. (CT 15) Appellant was found guilty as charged. (CT 143-145; RT 2:231-232) Appellant was sentenced to the midterm of 4 years, credit for 49 days precommitment confinement, including 16 days conduct credit.[1] (CT 148-149; RT 2:D-5-D9) Appellant filed a timely notice of appeal from the judgment. (CT 150) The judgment was affirmed in a published opinion by the Second District Court of Appeal, Division Five, in Case No. B216712.

---

[1] Petitioner was also sentenced for violating probation in Case No. BA340686, a violation of Health and Safety Code section 11359, to two years in prison, to run concurrent. (RT 2:D-8)

www.ingramcontent.com/pod-product-compliance
Lightning Source LLC
Chambersburg PA
CBHW030452220526
45464CB00006B/2498